I Know a Horse

– By Ernst Louis –

Illustrated by Evgenia Dolotovskaia

Publisher: Free Sparrows Kids, an Imprint of RelaSonship LLC

Dacula, GA 30019

Written by Ernst Louis

Design Concept by Ernst Louis

Illustrated by Evgenia Dolotovskaia

ISBN: 979-8-9857421-8-3 (Paperback)

ISBN: 979-8-9857421-9-0 (Hardcover)

Library of Congress Control Number: 2022913004

Fun Facts About Horses derives from information obtained from the website of

The British Columbia Society for the Prevention of Cruelty to Animals (BC SPCA).

I know a horse
who likes ice cream;

she's mine of course,
but in my dream.

This horse of mine
is tall and big;

she's only nine
and wears a wig.

I call her Nance; she's so unique!

she loves to dance

She likes to think,

and she can draw,

but she can't drink–
using a straw.

She is well read,
she's very smart;

When she eats bread—

it makes her fart.

Her favorite snack
is carrot sticks;

she has a knack for doing tricks.

She wins first place at the horse shows;

her silly face—
the whole town knows.

She loves to run
and loves to play;

she's so much fun
in every way.

Fun Facts About Horses:

Horses have the ability to sleep–
while steadily standing still;
their balance they are able to keep,
be it in their stall, or on a hill.

They have what is called **stay apparatus;**

it allows them to lock their limbs in place.

Tendons, ligaments, and muscles collaborate,

gifting them all with this amazing grace.

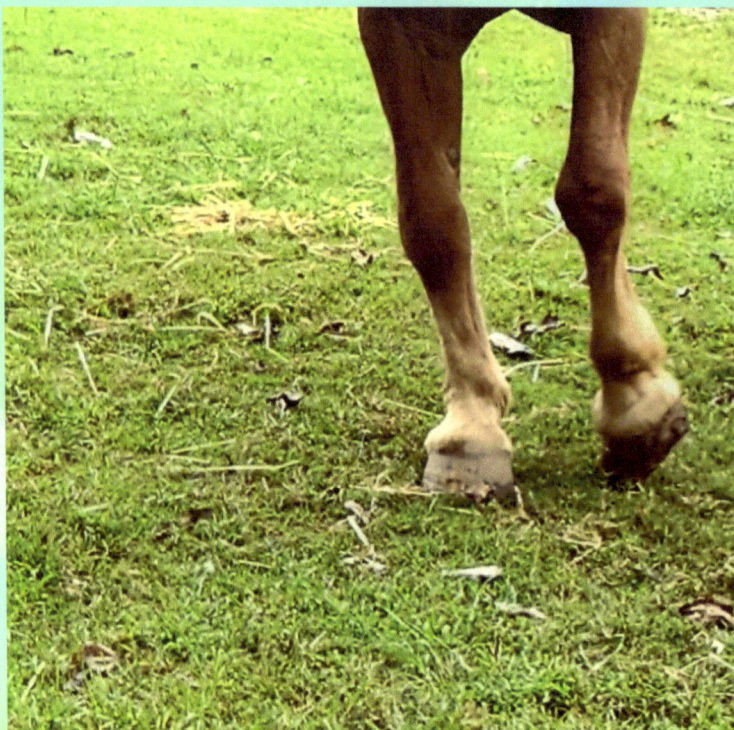

Obligate nose breathers,

horses are known to be;

breathing only through the nose–

is part of their physiology.

Horses have ten muscles in their ears,

humans have only three;

their ears can turn almost 180 degrees–

and what a cool thing to see!

"Horses will sometimes neigh

simply to attract attention.

This could be a sign of social isolation."

That's what horse Nance would say.

Horses can see almost all things around them.

I bet they would make awesome spies.

Precisely placed on the sides of their head–

are their very impressive, lovely eyes.

To all my precious, young readers around our beautiful, blue globe, you are amazing and I love you.

Dedicated to my lovely daughter, Maranatha. Dedicated also in memory of Bashert, the horse pictured below, rescued by Save the Horses, an organization located in Gainesville, Georgia. Bashert's name is Yiddish, and it means Destiny. To learn a bit more about Save the Horses and how you can support this important work, visit savethehorses.org.

Ernst Louis is a poet, children's author, graphic designer, and entrepreneur who resides in Dacula, Georgia–a suburb of Atlanta. He enjoys nature-walking, gardening, baking and lots of coffee. His cherished purpose as a writer is to inspire, educate, entertain, and uplift his readers. Ernst believes that kindness makes you awesome, and nothing beats awesome!

Evgenia Dolotovskaia was born and raised in Tbilisi, Georgia. She had been working as a graphic designer for 8 years when she decided to change her profession after giving birth to a baby girl. Her goal as an illustrator is to help authors visualize their thoughts and communicate with children through her art. She loves to travel the world to experience new cultures.

To request an author visit, or to order signed copies, go to freesparrows.com.

Other titles by Ernst Louis:

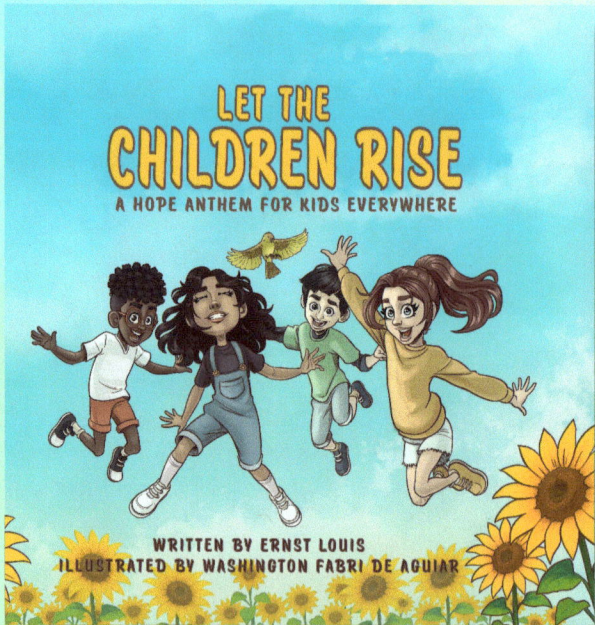

LET THE
CHILDREN RISE
A HOPE ANTHEM FOR KIDS EVERYWHERE

WRITTEN BY ERNST LOUIS
ILLUSTRATED BY WASHINGTON FABRI DE AGUIAR

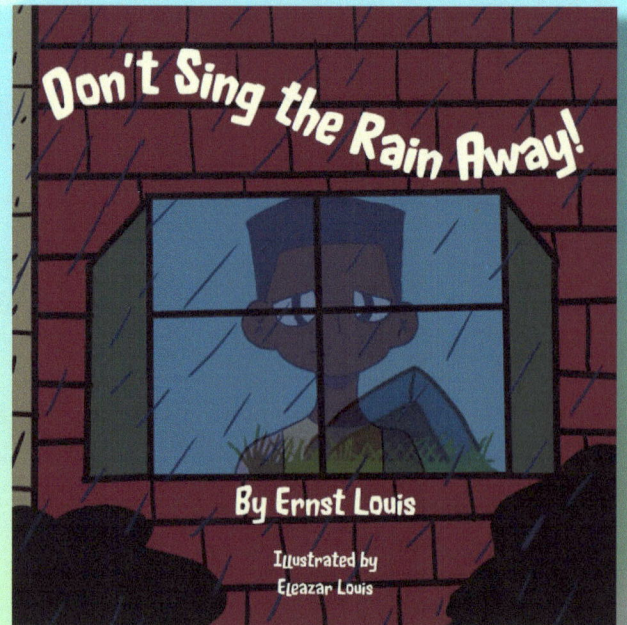

Don't Sing the Rain Away!

By Ernst Louis

Illustrated by
Eleazar Louis

If you and your little reader have enjoyed any of my books, please consider writing a review on Amazon to let others know what you think. This would be quite helpful. Thank you. :)

www.ingramcontent.com/pod-product-compliance
Lightning Source LLC
Chambersburg PA
CBHW041547260326
41914CB00016B/1570